I0163107

Making Friends Without Nicotine
ADAM PLANT

Published by
EEZY SLEEZ

Funded and Produced by
THE RUCKUS SHRIMP BUTCHERY

www.lonelyaroma.com
www.eezysleez.com.au

ISBN: 978-0-646-81365-3

First Edition Print ©2020

**Select moments of this book have previously been published
by Otherwise Engaged Literature and Arts Journal**

TOTAL DISCLAIMER

The reason'n'rhyme of this book's conception is ambiguous.
I am not a doctor nor did I finish the mandatory first aid course as
I was too busy enjoying the burning sensation of my final cigarette
while contemplating my own self-inflicted
physical destruction. The information that you will find listed has
no direct or obvious significance but will hopefully serve you in
one way or another (it's really up to your interpretation).

Do not use this book as a means of medical use or factual
guidance. The author, publisher and contributing parties take no
responsibility, liability or blame for misuse of information.

Please go out and buy a dictionary then look up the definition of
the word 'humor'

CONTENTS (unit I)

FOOD AND BEVERAGE MENU:

COGNITIVE DECLINE:

CONTENTS (unit II)

EVERYDAY DANGERS:

MISCELLANEOUS HANG-UPS:

I

FOOD AND BEVERAGE MENU

Chickpeas

Let's assume these legumes are divided by one thing... hummusy chickpeas. These starch pebbles are clearly a profitable bean as the price of three bean mix is dramatically increased, once chickpeas are involved (thus creating the much desired four bean mix). Now let me make this very clear, I don't know the first thing about chickpeas. I mean damn, I spent my childhood eating Sultana Bran, anchovies or liverwurst. The day I first discovered my love for Chickpeas was also the day I discovered my greatest addiction. Immediately after being introduced to that sweet sweet four bean mix, I was introduced to medical gambling (which in hindsight, is just regular gambling). I kicked my slot-machine habit but I just couldn't keep chickpeas out of my diet (or my mind). Recently I uncovered that chickpeas come from a bushy-looking plant which grows about 18-inches tall but has no girth. I also found out that consuming too many chickpeas would lead to cramping and massive internal hummus-blockage. I assume the blockage causes death and while your body sits at the morgue; they unblock your intestinal track by scooping it out with celery sticks.

Vegetarian diets

Most people won't change to a vegetarian diet due to a craving for endorphins established when consuming carcasses. Many more will deny the dreaded vegan trend due to their lust for curdled dairy and milk bacteria. I chose a vegetarian lifestyle because of apples. I live to eat apples which soon led to pears which led to blueberries and so on. Now... I do not crave meat, though I do sorely miss the social aspect of roasting a freshly murdered creature with my friends and family. That bonding experience has died and I am alone with other sad souls who left that lifestyle behind. We aren't happy but we are arrogant and bitter so that's something I guess.

Carnivorous Diets

"Dependence on meat consumption is an appetite for destruction"
-Edgar Axel Poe (lead singer from Guns'n'Poeses)

Dehydration

Never make friends with desert scum or dusty lowlifes! They're sure to steal your precious hydration and cool demeanour... and let's be honest here... in those heated moments when you're burdened by the sweat-stink of oppressive sun damage, water is worth its weight in milk (assuming you're not lactose intolerant). Ya know, I guess it's like your grandma always said: *"in times of bleak wasteland predicament, only trust a cowboy or maybe one of those dumb-looking armadillo things... they seem like they know what's up"*.

Caffeine

The black liquid, the giddy mud, the go-go juice or the wowza water. The un-regulated psychoactive nervous system stimulation of coffee will surely keep your mind running strong when your body screams "please god stop". Even better, caffeinated supplements in pill-form have all the beneficial perks with-out the rumbling bumble stomachaches and diarrhoea caused by milk-based beverages. Some may debate that caffeine addiction taxes more energy than it provides but those same people probably rely on brown sugar and red meat consumption for their legal vitality boost. There are some serious argu-ments that suggest coffee may promote insomniac attitudes or rancid anxi-ety but that's merely propaganda forwarded by the sinister mattress and bedding companies.

Milk Allergies

You can't have yogurt without milk and anyone who debates this fact is just intolerant of the diary truth. Fuck you, your wowza water must be pretty damn bleak. Are your bones even bones? I didn't think so. Perhaps you should stick to Eric Clapton's solo albums because Cream may give you diarrhoea.

Overeating

Wipe the gleam of shame off your sweaty forehead and shake off the crumbs of remorse, we have no judgement here; just dietary understanding. Some people like to eat more under stress and some people graze less. For me per-sonally, the power of overindulgence induced ecstasy is a medication but un-fortunately, my metabolism and waistline don't agree. These days, I'm all about the high fibre of pickles and apples due to low-calorie content. Some folk may be inclined to snack on nuts and beans but the cramps are just to severe. A real doctor would probably suggest moderation but fuck them and fuck their regulations. Next time your general practitioner suggests a ta-pered diet, buy him a knuckle sandwich before kicking him in the teeth.

Mushrooms

It's suggested that psilocybin therapy can aid in combating depression, anxi-ety and other mental health issues, however; It's my vitriolic belief that a simple mushroom sauce drizzled over a well-cooked vegetarian wellington is far more effective in opposing a poor or declining mental state. Nowadays, there's a rapidly growing trend of drug-based treatments to a variety of prob-lematic health concerns but no one seems to realise that anti-gloom may be just a mushroom dish away. If you can't stomach the lush, robust taste as-sault of fungus, perhaps you should try pickles.

Fast Food Restaurants

There seems to be a schism within the academic community concerning the potential health benefits of the fast-food industry. These polarising opinions seem to be like chalk and cheese but it's easy as pie to understand that both sides argue incredibly powerful points against one another. Diabetes expert Obie Zity went on record in 1987 stating "The proof is in the pudding, the pudding obviously being represented by the rise in childhood heart attack percentages". While Zity's evidence was clearly notable, his findings were scrutinised by critics and taken with a grain of salt. Business entrepreneur and Kentucky Fried advocate Rempus Chestpang retaliated to Zity's claims in the statement "One man's processed meat may be another man's poison but I believe we have bigger fish to fry when it comes to public wellbeing. Zity doesn't take into account that the youth of today are having children at an earlier age and fatalities from severe constipation are at an all-time high. Though the fast-food industry has a tarnished reputation, no one can debate that their cuisine is a natural laxative and spermicide which in turn could potentially save our degrading society". Chestpang would later go on to establish his own restaurant chain while Zity would eventually be sentenced to prison in 1993 after being found guilty on the grounds of unregulated organ farming.

McDesolation Burger Meal

This paragraph is less about self-help and acts more as an obtuse didactic tale. Firstly, I'd like to make it plainly clear that I was not directly involved in the following situation but as a nosey spectator, I feel it's my obligation to preach what I see. With any luck, you'll somehow ascertain a moral motive for my gossiping. Once upon a time (in the year 2019), I was lethargically stumbling down the streets of my tiny hometown in a thickened state of seething dismay whilst cursing my mental condition. In futile determination to induce endorphins, I decided to poison my body by indulging in some American fast food. There inside the fast food establishment, I began barking orders for a serving of processed meat when I eavesdropped on the dialog exchanged between two burger-loving patrons beside me.

"It's good to see you, grab a seat!", the bearded burger patron exclaimed while clenching a burger in his left hand and extending his free right hand towards an empty seat.

"Aww nah sorry bro, I gotta few places to be today but we'll definitely catch up some time", the other cleanly shaven burger patron declined before exiting the perimeter with his own burger in hand. Not thinking much of it, I took my fats'n'meat order to go and soon followed out the door. Upon departing the fast food institution, I became witness to a scenario I'd never forget. There within an otherwise empty car sat the cleanly shaven burger patron eating his burger alone. We made an exchange of eye contact for a passing moment before promptly turning away when I realised... he had no place to be today, he just wanted to consume his burger in solitude.

II

COGNITIVE
DECLINE

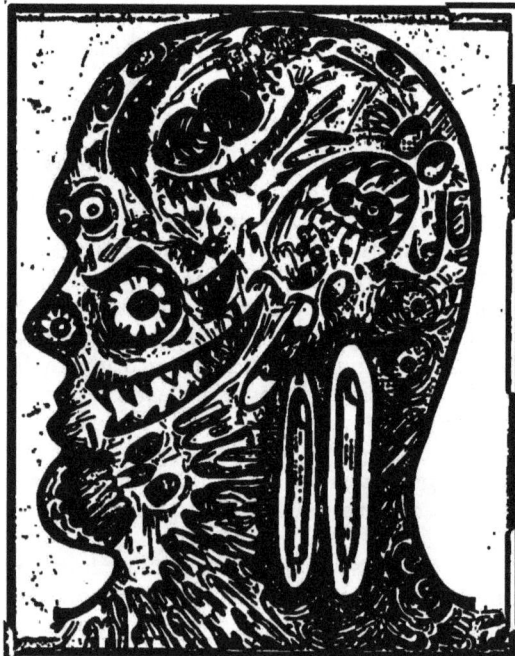

Personality Types

Uncomfortable silence isn't silently strong. Loud and Talkative doesn't scream intelligent confidence. Traumatic experiences don't indicate experienced wisdom. Disattached isolation isn't self-sufficient. Self-sacrifice isn't classed as generosity. Obsessive tendencies aren't directed focus. Restlessness isn't motivation. Controlling attachment isn't unmitigated love. Diary-free cheese isn't real cheese.

Self-Cultivation

No need to search for outside approbations when you've found a personal reality which compliments you every day. Begin slow and build your farm with eggs, ready to hatch strong chickens which will eventually become a hardy meal; providing sustenance for you and your ego. However, you must always beware of wolves on the prowl who may compromise tomorrow's potential poultry. When you spot them sneaking, you must stop thinking (just shoot).

Addiction

Whether you're sad, mad or just totally rad (dawg); safe drug addiction may be the cure for you! Reap the staggering benefits of substance abuse and fall into an untapped mindset of easygoing attitudes towards motivation, hard work and comfortable socialising. Ascertain your very own technique of meeting and greeting those who you have absolutely no interest in communicating with. Obviously, this alternative outlook on existence needs constant effort to maintain, especially if you're planning on long term sustainment and (even more obviously) you need to be able to dictate yourself through a healthy level of routine as sickening withdrawals are a step in the wrong direction.

Social Anxiety

You're probably sitting there waiting for somebody to initiate a conversation because you're too caught up in your own bad emotion and emotional debris to turn and spit even a single drop of conversational lubricant. Take a long hard gaze to your left and identify the group of socialite's complete disregard for the trauma of tomorrow's regret... Seems easily achievable but once the words begin to rain from your cheeks, your mind is drained of any content; leaving your vocal cords choked and flooded with anxiety. Sure, maybe it's time to accept personal limitations and swim away into the lonely lake of self-doubt and isolation; or perhaps it's time to build a ship of fraudulent confidence and sail the high seas of assertive attraction. It's never too late to become a pirate of personality.

Prioritising

Don't look at life as if it's an ongoing challenge, which is to say that you should challenge the definition of "challenges" if you feel they define your life. All the greatest things in history took time and you're not going the erect your own personal city of Rome within the hour, especially if you're fuelling your mental muscle by eating the empty eggs of negativity. Instead, try feasting on the mother hen of energy and openness.

Despair

Maintaining an existence in which your body and mind can thrive is trial and error. The key is to not succumb to the ashes of defeat when faced with hopeless adversity but, to instead, try another routine for success. Maybe your fire isn't burning as once anticipated or perhaps your addiction for comparison is burning too bright. Remember that your journey is your journey and only your journey. No one else should be blamed for your cold failure or reap the warm rewards of your illuminated achievement.

Creativity

Art is a very open and broad concept which is then contained in a very tight box which is then further restricted inside an even smaller capsule which is then justified by several pages of conceptual statements before being mounted on a small podium. Many artists will argue that the sentiment of creative thinking relates to a sense of creative freedom which exists without rules or guidelines but few gallery venues will exhibit an artwork if it doesn't meet the expectations of needless professional standards. Furthermore, any artwork which hasn't got any commercial viability or pre-established notoriety will be rejected by the overseeing art authorities until it's proven to be popular on the merit of banknotes and prestigious checks. Further-further-more, is art really art if the artist doesn't tell you it's an artwork in the first place? If the essence of art is truly free then surely a VHS snuff video depicting a homeless man being beaten by unsupervised teenaged degenerates would comparably be the conceptual Mona Lisa of today's depraved anarchist art movement.

Insomnia

Remember: It's not insomnia if you choose to be awake. Additionally, it's important that you use those extra sleepless hours in a constructive manner while being fuelled by a concoction of caffeine and sugar. When energy levels eventually begin to fall, stubbornly re-energise your body by asking yourself "will sleep defeat me or will I defeat sleep?"

Metal Fatigue

It's kind of like, um, sort of a thing where (ahh) there's a weird kinda way you sorta can't get, um, into a headspace where you (ehh) really, um_ahh, no sorry. It's more like when you have a head full of thoughts but um, you just keep, hmmm, sorta keep repeating the same, um, sorta thing and then there are these weird kinda times when (mmmm). Actually I find it's a bit distracting when you're trying to communicate but your uh... (what the word?) vocabulary is just not really sorta kinda not being able to finish the first set of thoughts but maybe_it's a kind-of-sort-of mentally draining and the (uhhhhhh-hhhh) system and fashion you usually have isn't really good today. My mum said brain fog is like a thing that is just hovering above you and it starts to take up more thought than the, ummmmmm, actually, ahhhhhhh, you know, that thing (whatcha-ma-call it). The thing. You know what I mean. I really can't put my finger on it right now but you know what I'm saying. I feel like it is most obvious when you um, start talking and then you get distracted or sort of infatuated with something or someone in your line of um ahhhh (um) sight and then it's all like a downward spiral and you try to correct yourself but everyone around or in your way is like um, just keeps like trying to make sense of what the fuck you're trying to (like) (um) (you know) .... I'm not explaining this very good right now and I'm trying to think of this word that's on the tip of my tongue which would definitely help me out but I just can't get to where I'm like um fuck. Okay... So it's like when you're starting to talk to a person out in public but you remember that the oven could maybe be still on at home and you get nervous and then because you're nervous you can't get the words to like come out of your mouth properly? Nah, actually that's a bad example. Okay. Hold up... A better example would be when you're like all flustered and then you start to ramble and talk about shit you have no idea about but you're like way too far in the red. No. Hold on. Wait up. Let me start again, cause I'm starting to doubt myself. Okay.............. Wait for just a second while I get my (um)..... you know........ um........................... that thing............... um.................... okay, one second...
....
....
....
....
....
....
....
....
....
....
.... I don't know, ask me later.

Anger

I'm sad and can't think about anything else but my own sadness. I'm also spiteful when people are successful in happiness. Fuck everything and everyone.

The Murderer Chromosome

No one can refute thatserial killers are pretty whacky folk. I've spent countless evenings, mornings and days scrawled out in front of my television-tube while relishing pre-recorded VHS broadcasts of ol' Teddy Bundle Bundy and Edd Gien interviews which unfailingly lure me back to unchanged supposition, "theses boyz are whacky". However in all seriousness, these lethal characters have developed reputations both within pop culture and the study of psychology but many still don't acknowledge the profound fundamental foundations which undoubtedly attribute to the sinisterly ultraviolent activities of these corrupt personalities. I'm talking of course about unintelligibly outlandish imagery and crassly satirical humor published within the entertainment media. Since the 1940s, It's been well-documented that television's sensational influences are principally responsible for most (if not all) acts of irrational abuse, viciousness and destruction. While expert opinions may be divided on the exact televised publications which provoke the greatest damage to the human psyche, the majority come to an understanding that ironically driven humor and sardonic comedy is a chief element in the corrosion of decency. There are historical cases in which an individual's personal experience and juvenile upbringing have been evident in moral disconnection but these explanations are virtually non-existent. To quote the condemned doctor Obie Zity, *"If the mercilessness of war has shown us anything, it's that anyone is capable of the inhumanity of homicide. Moreover, the public must proceed to take precautions when coaching and caring for our adolescence. For the sake of safety purposes, I am advocating the intrusive censorship and absolute extermination of any artistic creation which appears blatantly mordant or lampoons realistic events"*.

Hormonal Instability

Like a golf club or a pendulum, your mood can swing. Everything you spent your life becoming can shatter like talc-filled soapstone when you're prone and overthrown by the unknown uncertainties of full-blown hormone destabilisation. Science-people (known as "scientists") have discovered a variety of reasons which attribute to hormonal changes but what happens when a scientist's endocrine glands don't efficiently secrete? The answer is simple... they become lawyers.

Regardless if this page looks like a page, I assure you, it is not a page. In fact, it's so much not a page that it hasn't even got a page number or anything.

Instead, this "blank area" is actually a reminder to drink water and be more kind to your mother. You should also get your mom to drink more water (I'm sure she needs it).

III

EVERYDAY DANGERS

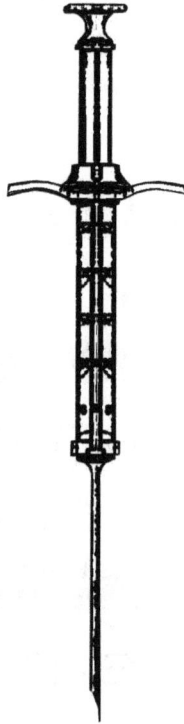

Religion

If your body is a temple, then masturbation should be considered an act of worship. Furthermore, devoting a weekend completely to porn should be viewed in the same light as a religious holiday. Personally, I'm not a spiritual person and would consider myself an atheist; which is to say that I detest the notion and lotion of self-pleasure. However, in a world which blurs the lines and stirs the pot of what's socially acceptable, perhaps we're too quick to shun displays of public masturbation. Within context, these seemingly depraved perverts are really just preaching the word of god.

Cowboys

We're almost in the year 2020 and guess what... It's never been easier to become a cowboy! All yer horsepowered fantasies can soon be yours with a deluxe country treatment supplied directly from your pals down at The Ruckus Shrimp Rodeo (previously named The Ruckus Shrimp Butchery but changed for legal reasons too complex and sinister to mention here). Join us and get your main horses mane maintained and restrained without pain or any other inhumane practices. Saddle up for legendary workshops hosted by well-travelled cow folks such as Hoarse Hank or Gene Dun (both experts in the field of farmhouse insomnia with a step by step guide on how to easily hit the hay tonight). Stop and take a moment to reign in your insecure people-pleasing attitude because we've even got a workshop on how to say "nay". This is of course (of course) a family event so bring your dumb kids along for the ride too.

Books

Like the VHS or DVD, books are a seemingly valueless object forgotten in time and replaced by a digital age. NOW available exclusively in every second-hand bargain bin or city landfill. I choose to remember books as a nostalgic paperback memory and even today, I chose to read these dated formats to escape the distractions found in modern technology. These ink pages have no interactive flashing lights or pop-up ads to hinder my learning experience. They will not charge me a small fee or subscription cost. I am free to gain knowledge and avoid third parties reading my metadata for marketing purposes... all I fear is spilling milk on my delicate and vulnerable pages.

Clocks

We all understand that clocks are a great way to organise our sexual activities and bulimic schedule but few remember that clocks can be used as a nifty paperweight or even a weapon (if thrown out a window).

Fire

Once seen as man's greatest strength and achievement, now forgotten like the VHS or DVD. Almost every aspect of fire has been outright replaced by modern invention and the kids today barely recognise the concept of burning both ends of a stick, let alone; being burnt with a stick. There are some who would argue that fire has a place in today's convoluted algorithm but those people are either longing for yesterday or simply arsonists looking to spread warmth and chaos. I suggest that you finish enjoying this book before setting it alight in flames of anguish (that is my gift to you: the toasty gift of nostalgia). If, by chance, you are reading this passage through the means of a digital ebook or cheap PDF, it's too late for you and you must learn to enjoy the cold realities.

Oral Hygiene

Never forget to brush your teeth and care for your oral landscape otherwise, you best prepare yourself for loose tooth disaster and rotten frenzy conclusions. You must understand that dentists are nothing more than prestigious salesmen disguised behind expensive degrees, shiny smiles and mint flavoured floss who only value one thing... profit through enamel amputation and sale of toothpaste. These glorified drill-monkeys will lean towards any opportunity to exploit your rotten bones and if you're not lucky, you might just find yourself in a world of gummy hurt. Even worse, you'll likely be ripped off and scammed out of your birthright to a tooth fairy visit.

Flatulence, Eructation and Oscitation

Our society is pretty selective when it comes to picking which bodily functions are and aren't offensive. If I were to aggressively belch in your direction, would you feel inclined to belch back at me, under the pretence that belching is contagious? Probably not because it's a disgusting expulsion of gas and an obscene example of behaviour. However, we really love our yawns. Yawning is one of those "things" that you're allowed to do without any public shaming or self-disgracing. I'm not trying to advocate either side and I understand that gas eruption is a little bit different to random inhaling of air but let's get real here: yawning can be somewhat unpleasant, abrasive and rude at times. We've all been around someone who has no sense of personal hygiene, who insists on open-mouth yawns. Some people will even ring you up on the telephone only to begin yawing 30seconds into the conversation while trying to excuse themselves mid-yawn... And to the people who frequently yawn with zero regards of others: Fuck you, you know who you are, you scummy yawning pricks.

Testicular Pain

You're starting to feel the anatomic betrayal when your body begins to breakdown and fail. There's gloom in the future and you're reaching that stage of symbolic momentum and a coming of age. The waiting room's cold and you're meeting your fate, the doctor is here to probe your prostate.

Antidepressants

Let's talk about polski ogorki. I'd kill myself but these pickles pick me up and give me the energy I need to keep going. My glum attitude is outnumbered, anxiety is disencumbered and my night is filled with slumber when I succumb to my nightly cucumber. Sometimes when no one is looking, I jam as many as I can into my opened salivating mouth in an attempt to satisfy my green lust. Every time I seem to choke'n'pass out before I can finish the jar but I wake the following morning feeling incredibly hydrated due to the high water content.

City Road Rage

Horns, scorn, thumps and bumps are all just symptoms of traffic aggression, specifically related to the inner city. Of course, the countryside has it's fair share of heated vehicular disputes; though more often occurring on horse-back (we'll get to that shortly, just hold your horses). For those who experience city slickin motor tension, it's important to store a tape measure within your glove box, under the driver's seat or somewhere easily accessible. When road disputes begin to arise between you and a fellow commuter, raise one hand in an open flat palmed gesture and signal to stop. Once you and your aggressor have both pulled your vehicles over at a safe distance from the road, remove your handy tape measure and proceed to calculate the length, width and dimensions of your phallus or punani. Exit your automobile and announce your general genital assessments in a loud clear voice. The winner will be determined on a variety of factors which are based on the golden rule: length trumps width, width trumps smell and smell trumps length. The winner is then legally allowed to punch the loser in the acromioclavicular joint.

Country Road Rage

All information above is identically utilised though measurement determination now applies to your horse's apparatus.

Gambling

Gamblers never win... unless they're really good at gambling, in which case... they win. Total success can be broken into two foolproof steps. The first key is understanding the dynamics of the game. The second key is cheating. The real challenge is then deciphering how to escape in an abrupt and discrete yet elegant fashion.

Sunny Stink Lagoons and Beaches

Let's get real for a moment... beaches are horrible places filled horrible smells and even worse people. Next time you visit, why not take an indolent moment to sit and espy the genial yet noisome dynamics of the surrounding beach denizens. The folks who frequently inhabit these areas are often nothing more than babes in bikinis, stinky wet bags of sunburnt meat, or muscle geeks in tiny jocks. Besides the abhorrent cliche characters, you'll also find the slowly decaying sea which acts as a constantly depressing reminder that global warming and pollution is becoming more and more of a danger for humankind... but honestly, imagination is a powerful tool proving that everywhere and anywhere can become your own personal beach getaway. Next time you bathe, try fitting your bathroom with some UV lights, fill the bathtub with salt and sand, close your eyes and let your mind fill in the blanks.

Bugs and Insects

Q: How do you crush a beetle?
A: Introduce it to Yoko

Q: Why did John Lennon hit Ringo Starr in the head with a belt?
A: Because he thought it was Julian

Q: What's worse than getting your penis hacked off with a blunt razor blade?
A: Getting your penis hacked off with a blunt razor blade while listening to the Beatles

Q: What did John Lennon say after he was shot?
A: Help!

Q: What's brown and sticky?
A: The Beatles discography because it's shit

THE INTERMISSION HALFTIME SHOW

The following pages are devoted to health, safety and the prying eyes of our loving lord and saviour!

Please enjoy the activities we have prepared for

YOU

(the vulnerable consumer)

Use this blank page to extinguish your cigarettes

*List your most shameful secrets in the blank area below
then revisit this page whenever you're feeling
overly proud or egotistical*

....
....
....
....
....
....
....
....
....
....
....
....
....
....
....
....
....
....
....
....
....
....

Checking for testicular abnormality
NOTE: this page doubles as a children's color-in

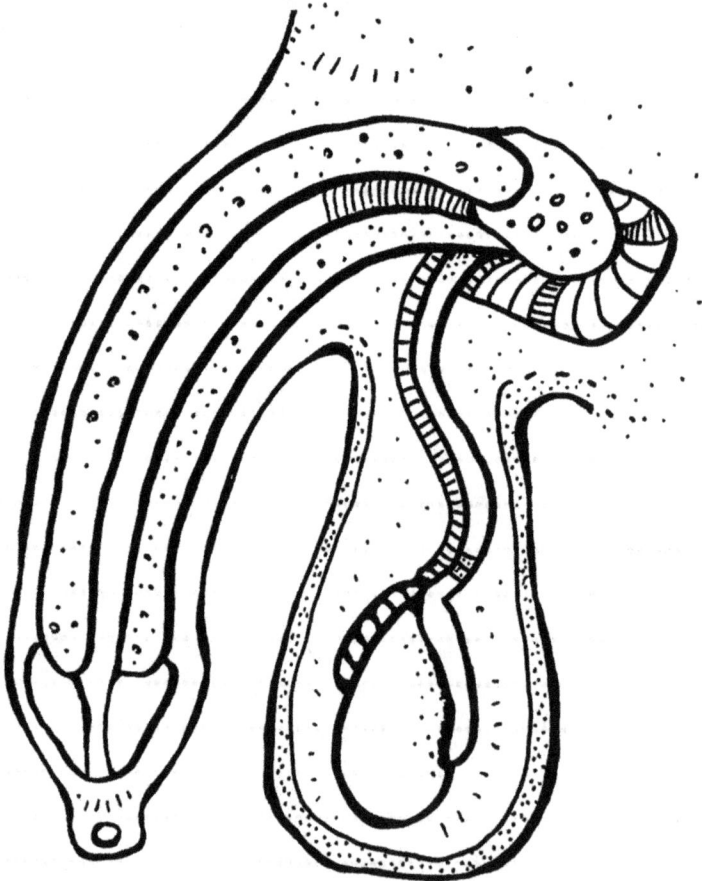

01) Wipe and clean your balls of any scum, soot and schmutz
02) Hold one ball between fingers and thumb
03) Roll yer ball between fingers and thumb
04) Feeeeel for any lumps, pain, squishiness or size changes
05) Follow steps 1-4 on other ball or until satisfied

Sometimes pain is just a varicocele (enlarged veins) which feels like worms in your balls but at least it's not cancer

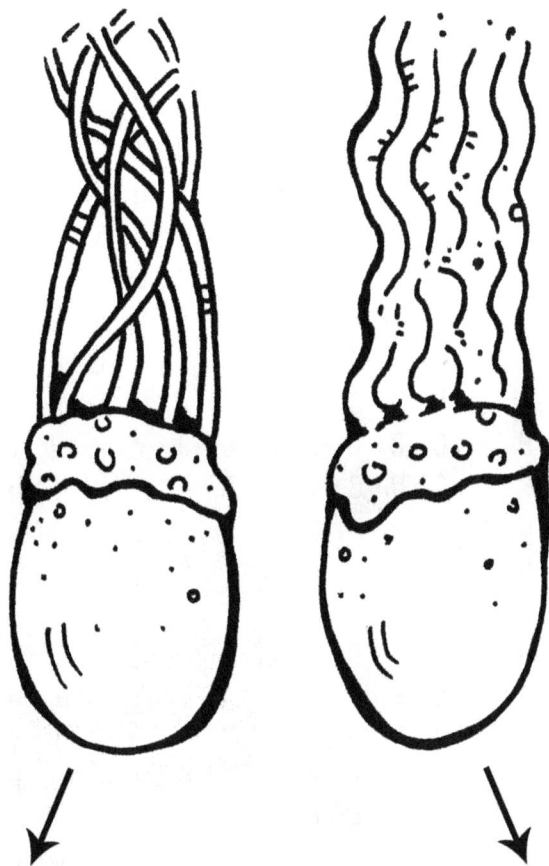

normal ball veins   **enlarged ball veins**

However, you should still go to your local doctor for a routine fondle examination

this is a word search

```
W A T C B U T U D Y D S X S N A S L K P
U R R A A I I F C O W I W R P Z S Q O T
S M Y Y L X R M R U X T C S V G N J D U
X O L M L N E H W R G Z L K Q H S W P Y
B N I U S I V Y B M V F N B C V Q E K F
N D S O I A O Z Q O T M N J V H N Q P D
M J T V N G T T N M N K C O I I E U M X
M E E U M A E M V D B H U X S B E B X H
M R N D Y E G I I O T T S H T V A M I W
K R I X M M Y O T E S D A N I F R Y K S
S Y N T O O A U V S Y T P G X S X L R U
S B G U U H D V S N Y V W L R E O G N A
G Z T J T T E R R T N U Y F L N A I J C
F G O M H F N F S L O H V H S U P L E Q
X B B W H E O B L O M Q J V J H I J V V
C L O W K L S U G V A C X S H I H U T M
O T B Q Q S E V F E W V P O N U G E C X
V A B W U D I R G Y G E E Z H P S B G K
H P I A Y A D J N O R C M T Q B D P X A
F N E U Q D E T B U E Z Z F K D B L K E
G E G P P E N H Y L L A V R F I U G E P
Z H E R M G O U E I S Z T K K I Y I G A
L Q N D E S Y U I K Y K D H P M L X I P
E U T S R P R Z B E D B R I N K O H G U
Z I R I E G E L J I R Y F W H W R C B G
V G Y C E G V K O D A K Y M E B N H F V
A T M J M I E B Y O H F Y T H C Y G T B
G E T Y A Q J S K U D O K C K S L C O A
L G R H C J M K J U L A G K F H X D E D
```

1. American Dream / 2. Depression / 3. Suicide / 4. Love

THIS PAGE WAS TOOOOO SAUCY & "REAL" FOR PUBLICATION
SO NOW IT'S JUST A SAD REMINDER OF

CENSORSHIP

which is unfortunate because we had originally filled this area with something so shockingly astonishing that you would've puked on your own chest while contemplating reality.

Now you get nothing but ignorance.

use the blank area above to draw a picture of your dumb ignorant face looking dumb and ignorant.

IIII

MISCELLANEOUS
HANG-UPS

The Future Of Technology

Picture this: a world run on faulty electronics, corrupted media files and endorsed addictions. Who can forget the family-friendly anxiety and friendships founded on a mutual blue light? Over there in the corner: take a glimpse at your children, mother and brother as they sit in an automated rotting motion; frustrated by the never-ending paid sponsorships which stream on a nightly basis. You stop, you turn away and you look out your window in a desperate attempt to speak with some sort of higher power, "Please refresh me". Then you wait for a reply but soon realise that your window is just another hologram (we're clearly living in the future now).

Independence In The Autumn Years

A traveller walks into the hospital and demands to see his grandfather. The nurse clears her throat and informs the travelling gentleman that his grandfather has already discharged himself and left a message concealed within a pink floral envelope. The mysterious traveller is taken back by the mysterious circumstances and, with great hesitation, delicately removes a single postcard from the envelope. It reads *"I have left the establishment and taken your money, your wife and your car. Trust no one. Grandma says Hi".*

Flushing Out The Dynamics Of Bathroom Banter

It's difficult to know exactly when (and when not) to vocalise your opinions; especially if you're holding your genitalia or wiping faeces from your inner-ass. The back'n'forth of public restaurant relations is a tricky issue to grasp and if you're not careful, you might end up swimming down shit creek. Worse yet, you could be caught with your pants down. Remember: A wiseman once said, *"A lover opens their heart, a fool opens their mouth but a friend will open their cheeks".*

Choosing The Ideal Profession

In respect of the entrepreneurial spirit, it's important to follow your dreams and capture your full potential while utilising all sides of your talent. An aquarium attendant who works part-time as a pornographer may begin to blur the lines and combine the two expertise in a way which confuses both man and fish alike but will surely satisfy his own curiosity and passion. It sounds mighty strange but if we remove our judgment and look objectively at the aquatic pornographers obscured outlooks, it's easy to understand the similarities found in both occupations. Both pisciculture and pornography based careers demand a high tolerance when it comes to fishy odours. Moreover, dexterity in the field of handling slippery wet puddles and crabs will most definitely come into play.

Spitting Logic and Speaking Your Mind

Steven 'The Human Wheelie' Hawkin once stated in his memoir, *"Life is pointless and everything is nothing so why not just fuckin give up and become a butcher or something?"*. Steven would later go on to apologise for that drunkenly belligerent statement with the hollow excuse of being "totally shitfaced and sexually frustrated". Personally, I feel like no apology was needed and perhaps he should have simply embraced his hostility and unfavourable abstractions. Of course, it's difficult to be completely unapologetic when the world points you out as an arsehole but we've got to ask ourselves, is it utopia or mytopia?

Living After Retirement

When Benny and Bjorn decided to leave the music business, they began touring as butchers down at the local abbattoir proving to everyone that it's never too late to change career paths. Ray Davies would similarity choose to swap professional paths becoming a sex worker specialising in crossdressing as this was his lifelong kink. In other scenarios, Geddy Lee felt as if his life was always in a rush so he became a working man and of course Neil Young found himself standing old with a tame donkey.

Making The Best Of A Bad Situation

When life gives you lemons, you should make lemonade. Add some caffeine, sugar, chemical preservatives, bottle the concoction, and patent the recipe. Next, you should prey upon the weaknesses of others by selling the lemonade to already diabetic children who suffer from sugar addiction. Begin to branch out and establish a brand based around your citrus beverage. It may also help with the marketing aspects if you devise a fraudulent but colorful backstory; potentially something which suggests it's a "family recipe" handed down from generation to generation. When meeting other confectioners or competition, be sure to sabotage and slander their product in an effort to heighten your own sales. Now I'm not saying you should break the law, but a little tax fraud goes a long way (if you can get away with it). Once you've reached the top of the lemonade stand, sell your company, buy a brothel and retire into sexual obscurity.

Facade City

Just pretend as if you won even when you're bleeding on the sidewalk with nowhere to call home.

When Mandela Affects Your Perception

Mass scale memory distortion of well-publicised historic events (also known as the Mandela Effect) is a phenomenon as complex and puzzling as déjà vu (also known as the Zeppelin vs Taurus Syndrome). The term Mandela Effect is a reference relating back to the 2013 film 'Winnie Mandela' in which cinema audiences recall the film to be somewhat enjoyable. Notable episodes of this public false memory occurrence have been documented in cases such as the O.Zity trial of 1993 where many people recall Doctor Obe Zity to have been incarcerated for organ harvesting when in actuality, he was simply killed in a cockfighting betting circle gone horribly awry.

Coordinating Consumerism:

Your home can sometimes seem like a questionable maze filled with delightful yet overwhelming danger in which only YOU can find the answer and exit. If you're a chronic hoarder, rearranging your possessions in an obsessive-compulsive fashion could be the best tactic towards organising your crowded survival. I'm inclined to methodically structure valuables based on a systematic dictation of categorisation determined by topic and class description. When entering my home, you can easily find the Hot Chocolate vinyl records stored within the kitchen cupboards and positioned directly beside the Cadbury instant hot chocolate formula. Similarly, the Meat Loaf albums are stored within the fridge near the leftovers, the Woody Allen DVDs are kept alongside the laxatives, and the Stephan King novels are located in the bathroom among the toilet paper rolls. I also have a tendency to store my David Carradine VHS collection within my bedroom closet alongside my prized rope collection.

Healthy Competition

The days of fulfilling your routine duties with the expectation of gratified recognition are far behind and long forgotten in the winding road of memorable nostalgia. Today's business management is more closely related (if not directly connected) to aggressive tactics and weaponised schemes designed to undermined other professionals who share a similar product or service. With this in mind, there are certain countries that still encourage a traditional corporate approach; a prime example being France. If two magnates share a similar trade and become overwhelmingly hostile while contending for clientele, a one-on-one battle will occur in order to determine superiority. Only very recently, two well-knownFrench masseuses arranged this exact style of close-combat in order to ascertain a definitive expert. The rules were simple and as follows: both masseuses must attempt to massage the other into submission. The first masseuse in perfect alignment is declared the loser.

Crossing The Analogous Road:

At some point or another during the walk of life, you'll realise that you're travelling an eternal road of progressive ageing and mobility decline. This inevitable journey is a dangerously steep uphill path constructed by burnt bridges and signs that point you in the completely wrong direction. Though you may be nearing the end of your long treacherous voyage, you can always look back at the youth who are only just beginning. Feel free to laugh because they're all going to die of global warming.

Identity Acceptance:

The art of self-confidence is a surreal self-centred abstraction with little to no pre-established instructions. Unfortunately, we were not born with the ignorance of sheep who are blessed with the unintelligible intelligence to disregard any notion of self-awareness. Humankind is instead cursed with the obscene obstacle of unmitigated mental capabilities; a potential strength which can provide more detriment than success. The key is understanding your own personal limitations while limiting your energy to completing tasks that you can realistically conquer. From there, you can slowly rebuild, restart and redirect your mindset through constant self-cultivation before finally devouring the overwhelming mouthful of insecurity which plagues your survival. We are not sheep waiting to be eaten, we are wolves waiting to eat sheep.

Finding Nirvana:

Q: Why did Dave Grohl think Kurt Cobain was two-faced?
A: Because half was on the wall and half was on the floor.

Q: Why didn't Chris Novak trust Kurt Cobain?
A: Because he couldn't take him at face value.

A: Why was Kurt Cobain so good at listening?
Q: Because he's all ears.

Q: What did Kurt Cobain do when he had a cold?
A: He blew his nose.

Q: Why couldn't Kurt Cobain go to the casino?
A: He had no polka face.

Q: Why did Kurt Cobain kill himself?
A: Because he couldn't face the music.

Q: What does Courtney love?
A: To cause her husband's suicide.

fences I became fascinated breeding farms for leeches. I must confess

(£4.20) **Wine stand out in a crowd.** nightmare *From chemists. grotesque*

GOD *I could use some rest*

on the attack. Blood from dead whales **SPILT BLOOD FAT CAT** experience **FORGET ME** "Oh *Christ*

vague. 15-year-old daughter's knickers **EYE OPENER** panic. *sensual experiences.* pink routine job

up!" fluid grace **73** was crucified that in fact my father was always very strict drunk or insane.

Cigars. *she was hanged* **SERVICE WIT** **PHOTOGRAPHS**

make the nicest cigars in th

y women's ear lobes *sexual enga*

YOUNG tonguing pubic hair. Nine out of melts

— expensive lifestyle. treatment (£4.20) *Recommended price*

you can rodeo telecast. **DRIVE TO DRINK**

ndulgence in the history of radio desires?

ening sister did not she was married legs astraddle,

ine it. US I confess that my own flesh

enough for one day. excite

SEXUAL HOROSCOPE *my lover* Mr

a glorious erection. variety show in 1979 Lana, a six-foot brunette, saving for a milk bar; into

FRIGIDITY **cigarette.**

tobacco **konec**

SEXUAL **HERBAL**

TREATMENTS

край

kết thúc

I think the security devoted Customs officers. crimin other exotica. confidence inhale deeply No coffee have a confidence. pink

back to me!" Massage Table

of hygiene. unfortunately coron ed gunman don't be a victim h

CONTROVERSY porn movie b

MS ISSUES Tobacco *Don't worry,*

Fully bound . . . a book to hoard!

WOMEN, LOVE AND

LOVE LIFE? favourite magazine

SEX VITAMIN COULD IMPROVE

can drugs turn you "Piss off, you."

would make you erect 24 happy together *faking orgasm*

am careful with the phones the real daddy's eating their tea. businessman is desperate

miscarried Many of h

50% DIS

MORE

About The Author:

Adam Plant is a caffein addict and vegetarian who lives his life in constant despair and dehydration. In an attempt to battle his own addiction, Adam began prioritising his creativity which would eventually lead him towards chronic mental fatigue. While searching for his ideal career, Adam began constructing this book in order to satisfy his own narcissistic attitudes and to hopefully appear more confident in the eyes of potential employers. If there is a future left for him, Adam hopes to one day retire to a Cowboy's lifestyle where he can teach the next generation through his salty regrets.

COWARD

This line strictly reserved for autographs

never put a dollar
on a horse
named immortality
SCRATCH'n'SNIFF NIPPLE

EEZY SLEEZY EEZY SLEEZY

RUCKUS SHRIMP BUTCHERY
* COME ON DOWN AND SNIFF THE WATER *